Don't Worry Sweet Child
A Book On Angels
By Caroline Farinelli Aronson
Illustrated by Ros Webb

To my daughter Sofia, this book is for you sweet girl!
You have taught me more than you will ever know.
I hope that you always follow your dreams and worry less
because you know that your angels are always with you!

Published in the United States by CFA Ventures LLC, Mechanicsburg, PA
Copyright © 2022 by Caroline Aronson. All rights reserved.
Cataloging-in-Publication Data is on file with the Library of Congress

Hardcover ISBN: 979-8-9858801-0-6
Paperback ISBN: 979-8-9858801-1-3
Ebook ISBN: 979-8-9858801-2-0

Illustrated by Ros Webb
Printed in the United States of America

Don't worry sweet child,

you need to believe.

There are angels among us

you just cannot see.

When you call upon them,

they will always be near.

Ready to listen

and take away fear.

You can ask them for guidance

whatever you need.

Just call out their names

and you will receive.

Archangel Michael,

is the angel of protection.

He will give you courage, and point

you in the right direction.

So if you are scared

or feeling lost.

Remember, call Michael

your fears will be squashed.

Books and movies are sometimes creepy.

This can be hard for you to feel sleepy.

But don't worry sweet child, you are protected.

When you close your eyes and go to sleep,

remember Michael is watching, no need to make a peep.

Bad dreams can happen

but don't be afraid.

Archangel Michael can help you be brave.

When you travel far

and are in a new place,

Angel Michael makes sure

you feel super safe.

SHOW & TELL
CARE FOR YOUR FISH
1. feeding
2. cleaning
FISH FOOD
FISH

Call on Archangel Gabriel

when you can't find the words.

He will comfort and guide you

until you feel heard.

If your teacher calls on you

to speak up in class,

you may feel you want to

be quiet and pass.

But don't worry sweet child you are loved.

Poster
Paint

Now that you know Gabriel is near,

he will come to the rescue

so you can speak loud and clear.

Writing and drawing are fun to do.

Gabriel is there to make sure

your ideas come shining through.

With your family and friends

you might all disagree,

but just turn to Gabriel.

He will set your words free.

When you are feeling unwell

call upon Archangel Raphael.

He will always be there

to come to your aid.

His power to heal

will never fade.

When you are scared to go to the doctor,

and you have to get shots,

all the scary pokes

can make boo boos hurt a lot.

Don't worry sweet child you are safe and alright.

Remember Raphael is beside you

to make cuts and bruises heal.

He'll help calm your nerves

so you don't have to squeal.

His healing is always around

for you and the ones you love.

Raphael will remind you don't worry,

and give you all a big hug.

Always remember that you are never alone.

Your angels can hear you

without using a phone.

Don't forget to talk with your angels

in cheerful times too.

Your joys will make them happy.

Your light will shine through.

Sometimes you might need your angels
right now.

So take a deep breath and look up to
the clouds.

Just let them know you need them,

and ask for their hand.

They will be there to guide you

and help you understand.

you are protected
you are safe
you are loved
you are safe
you are bright
you are protected
and along

Remember to repeat to yourself morning
and night...

You are protected,

You are loved,

You are safe and alright.

So when you've had a bad day

or you're feeling alone,

or your worries make you question

all the unknown...

Promise me you know this is not true.

Your angels are with you forever.

Now you know what to do.

Don't worry sweet child!